Beyond Office Politics

The Hidden Story of Power, Affiliation & Achievement in the Workplace

Linda Sommer

D1336112

TERMS OF USE AGREEMENT

TABLE OF CONTENTS

FOREWORD

*B*eyond *Office Politics: The Hidden Story of Power, Affiliation & Achievement in the Workplace* is a game-changer. This book will make visible to you something extremely important about yourself and others that has always been there. Once you see it, your career and your professional life, as well as your personal life, will make much more sense to you. This newly visible reality, together with what I am going to teach you about how to navigate it, will allow you to ask better questions, make more enlightened choices, and create much greater success for yourself.

You will find that doors to your success that once seemed inexplicably shut will now open. People that used to annoy or frustrate you will no longer have the same power over you that they once seemed to have because you will now see what is going on and know how to respond constructively. Most importantly, you will feel and be much more in control of your professional success.

All this because you will hold the key to the #1 Blind Spot in the workplace: how people (including you) position themselves through Power, Affiliation & Achievement.

- If you have ever been frustrated or put off by office politics, you need the information and skills presented in this book.
- If you have ever felt misunderstood or underutilized by your boss, you will learn why and what you can do about it.
- If you have had trouble managing your team or getting your employees to do what you need them to do, you will find most of what you need to know in the pages of this book.
- If you have a coworker or boss that you just can't seem to get along with, you really need to understand and apply what I will teach you in this book.

So why is positioning—together with the strategies and preferences we all have for positioning ourselves—such a blind spot? To answer that, we first have to know what creates a blind spot.

The most well known blind spot is the one you have to be aware of while driving. This blind spot is large enough for another car driving along next to you to be completely hidden from your view. That, as you know, is a significant blind spot, and it is created by the placement of your rearview and side mirrors. There is a gap in visual coverage that you have to compensate for by turning your head and looking where the mirrors can't see.

What creates a blind spot, then, is a feedback gap. Our car mirrors are providing a lot of feedback for what is behind and beside us while we are in our car, but there is a gap in that feedback. The information is incomplete.

In short, a blind spot occurs when the feedback information we have doesn't adequately cover the situation we are in. As we know from driving, this kind of feedback gap can really be dangerous. And usually it's not that the information is unavailable. In the car it's just a matter of turning our heads to fill in the information gap. What's really problematic, though, is when we don't know that we have a blind spot, and that is certainly the case for most people when it comes to positioning. And because we are so unaware of positioning, we fabricate all kinds of reasons and excuses to try and make sense of why things happen. "My boss doesn't like me." "She is just a difficult person." "He will throw you under the bus if you're not careful." And perhaps the most common explanation: "Office politics."

Why is positioning such a blind spot for us? For such a large blind spot to exist so universally, there have to be several factors at work simultaneously. And there are. The first reason we have this blind spot is precisely because positioning is such a universal and ongoing reality in all parts of our life. It's so everywhere all the time that we just don't see it. It's like asking the fish in the ocean about water. "Water? What water?"

Another significant reason for our positioning blind spot is that we tend to see things as we would like them to be, not necessarily as they are. For example, economists are currently realizing that they have had a blind spot about how consumers make decisions. It certainly would make things easier for economic forecasting if people made their economic decisions rationally, but the truth is much different. People have all kinds of reasons for making their economic decisions, and most of those are closer to emotional reasons than rational ones. In a similar way, we want to believe that cooperation is how we work together best—or how we should work together—and so we tend to skip over or look down on competition in the workplace. Yet competition, as a foundational element of positioning, is everywhere, especially at work.

A third extremely significant factor in our positioning blindness is that we have a tendency to believe that all people are like we are, or that they should be like we are. Those who truly are like us become our friends, and the rest often really surprise us with the choices they make. In general, we simply don't get or accept that people really do have different and complementary differences.

A blind spot about positioning is costly. Very costly. Especially in today's world of extreme competition and change, you need to be aware of your own and others' positioning styles, strategies and preferences. This book will do that and more for you.

I would also like to say just a few words about the origin of this material. The story that you are about to read is of course a piece of fiction, a modern workplace parable. Yet you will see yourself and others you know in this story because the dynamics of positioning are universally human. David McClelland, the Harvard psychologist, popularized the terms Power, Affiliation & Achievement, but the positioning styles they refer to have been known literally for ages. The Greeks, for example, used the concepts of logos, pathos & ethos (logic, feeling and authority) to identify the three ways that we persuasively position our messages to others. McClelland's gift was to put these social motivations in a modern context, and what I have done is create a story and supporting material that will teach you how to position yourself and establish productive rapport with your coworkers, bosses, and those in your charge. To do this I relied on the groundbreaking work of behavioral linguist Joe Yeager, who has taken our knowledge about language, motivation and decision making to new levels.

I promise you that what you will learn in this book is the foundation for a successful career in any field. The benefit you will receive from this knowledge is limited only by how well you learn and apply it. My years of coaching executives and professionals at the highest levels in the fields of finance, technology, marketing, entertainment, business, education, law and medicine have taught me that positioning is the #1 blind spot, and that this material is priceless. In the end, business is about relationships with other people, and your success will be determined by how well you build and maintain rapport with others. I know from experience that understanding the positioning styles of Power, Affiliation & Achievement will empower you to make the most of yourself and your talents—and give you the leverage you need for success.

ACKNOWLEDGEMENTS

T hank you Joe for your genius, your divine inspiration, your mentorship and your infamous anecdotes.

Liam, endless thanks for your writing expertise and creativity, but most importantly, your friendship, your untiring patience and your beautiful music. This book would never have happened without you!

Juliette, Lisa, Christophe – you are constant inspirations. Thank you for supporting me in this adventure and making the space so it could come to fruition.

Special thanks to my family for giving me a multitude of stories to pull from – our diversity certainly makes us special! Benjamin – you have been so supportive. Thank you.

Thank you to my team at Sommer Consulting whose professionalism and dedication makes every day a pleasure. Your desire to be your best and your encouraging feedback have been so important to me.

And last but certainly not least, thank you to all my clients, past and present, for allowing me to participate in your professional journey.

Chapter 1

HIERARCHY & POSITIONING

"If your current job were offered to you today, complete with everything you now know about it, would you take it?"

Don E., senior manager at BioWidgets, was out of the office. Not much else put a smile on his face these days, but as he went to refill his java at the Java Hut he felt pretty good. Just to get a break from all the office nonsense lifted his spirits. There was also just a touch of playing hooky to his unscheduled café time, and that reminded him of his more carefree days as a student. Fifteen years ago in college he never would have imagined all the b.s. he had to put up with just so that he could do his job. Thinking about the office again brought him down from his brief good mood, and he slowly made his way back through the café tables to his laptop and the reports he was working on.

A couple of tables over from his, Don noticed a book placed on a table. He could easily read the title: *Beyond Office Politics: The Hidden Story of Power, Affiliation & Achievement in the Workplace*. He paused. For quite a few years he had read every business success book he could get his hands on. Most had given him useful information of one sort or another, but none had really rocked his world.

"Any good?" he asked the older gentleman whose book it was.

"Why do you ask?" replied the gentleman, giving Don a genuine smile.

"I've always found those kind of books to be a disappointment. They seem great at first, but they don't have staying power."

"All sizzle, no steak?"

"Exactly." There was immediately something about this guy Don really liked, and he searched for something to say to keep the conversation going.

"Do you have a minute?" the gentleman asked, inviting Don to sit down. "We could talk about it. My next appointment seems to be running late."

Don found himself sitting down, and the gentleman introduced himself as Joe. They exchanged a few pleasantries about the café, and then out-of-the-blue, Joe asked Don a question that floored him.

"If your current job were offered to you today, complete with everything you now know about it, would you take it?"

Don was stunned. This guy Joe seemed to be some kind of mind reader. There was in fact a job he was in line for at Bio-Widgets, but there were two problems: Jack, the other front-runner for the job, and the fact that the new job seemed like it might just be an updated version of his current job—which he had come to realize he wasn't particularly cut out for. Well, actually he loved the work, he was a real wizard at biowidgetry, but the job itself was way too political for him.

"No," Don said resolutely. There was something liberating just about saying it out loud like that. "I wouldn't take it."

When Joe asked him why, Don went into detail about his impossible boss, then Jack the power-hungry new guy, and Casey, whom he had picked to run his core team but who was having trouble getting consistent performance out of them. The three of them were literally driving him to drink, even if it were only overpriced java.

"Do you mind if I cut to the chase?" Joe asked. "I may have a viewpoint that will help clarify a few things."

Don gave his assent. After all, what was there to lose? If this guy could help him see a way out of things, he'd take it, even buy his lunch.

Joe proceeded to draw some circles and lines on a napkin.

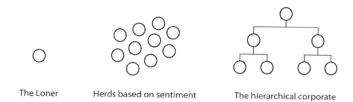

The Loner   Herds based on sentiment   The hierarchical corporate

"Basically," Joe began, "there are three types of mammals: solo, herd, and hierarchical." He then explained how solo mammals like bears and tigers live alone, except for at mating time. Herd mammals, on the other hand, like gazelles and cattle, also have no social structure but mingle around one another for safety in numbers against predators. Hierarchical mammals, however, like chimps, apes, wolves and humans, have an instinct for social organization. "This means," continued Joe, "that there are top dogs and underdogs." He explained that the most obvious example of ranking was the military, with a descending pyramid structure from generals to privates, and that other institutions, including the corporate business world, also have an organizational system that clearly defines rank and position to reflect hierarchical power.

Because of our hierarchical social instinct, Joe explained further, people are always "positioning" themselves for the highest position they can attain in the social organization. Much of our daily stress and conflict is therefore about how we continuously reposition ourselves. Some don't like to do positioning, some want a better position than they can achieve, some don't want to acknowledge positioning as a fact of life, and some take to positioning like a duck to water. But we all, Joe emphasized, want to be high up in position, and no one likes to be put down. "Denial of the realities of positioning causes much distress among those who do the denying," he added, pausing for effect.

Don considered what Joe was telling him. It was true that he had little patience for people, such as Jack, who openly played the "politics game." Power-hungry and brash, they really rubbed him the wrong way. People, Don believed, should be evaluated and compensated for their performance, what they produced. Everything else was secondary. He was willing to do his best, to continually improve his knowledge and performance, but he had no desire to glad-hand or maneuver his way up the ladder. His work would speak for itself.

"So what do you think?" Joe asked. He took a sip from his cup and looked over the rim of his glasses at Don.

"Power struggles and competition are innate, isn't that what you're saying?" Don asked.

"And success comes to those who know what game they're in and play it well," added Joe. His tone made it clear that he was referring to Don.

"I'm not sure I have the desire or the skills," Don said matter-of-factly, yet the emotion he suddenly felt surprised him.

"It sounds to me like you may have benched yourself before finding out," replied Joe. He smiled one of his good-natured, hearty smiles again and extended his hand. "It's been swell talking to you," he said. He handed Don one of his business cards, and Don wasn't too surprised to see that Joe's business was called Boardroom Executive Coaching. "Give me a call if you'd like to talk some more."

For the rest of the day, in fact the rest of the week, Don couldn't get his conversation with Joe out of his head. He even asked around a little and discovered that Joe—actually Dr. Joe—was something of a legend in the executive coaching business. The word was, he got results like no one else. But that wasn't why he decided to give him a call and ask for help. Two things had stuck with him, to the point that Don needed to know more. For one thing, his short lesson on hierarchical animals had hit home. Everywhere Don looked now he noticed the elusive obvious. People were always positioning themselves, in their clothes, in their language, in their cars, in their stories, in everything. Now he couldn't understand how he had missed it.

Not only that, but Don suddenly saw how people seemed to fall into the hierarchical, solo, and herd animal categories. How could this be? Hadn't Joe said that humans were hierarchical, with an instinct for social ranking and positioning? Yet Don clearly saw how he could group most of his coworkers and business associates clearly into one of these categories. Casey definitely seemed the group type—always going out to lunch with the gang or going to meetings it seemed she didn't really have to attend. Jack, on the other hand, was clearly hierarchical. Don imagined that Jack even had a map of "top dogs" and "underdogs" posted on a wall at home so that he could figure out whom to kiss up to and whom to cut off at the knees. As for solo animals, Don knew that he had to look no farther than the mirror to see a perfect specimen. At least at work, solo was his mode, his standard operating procedure. Even when he worked on projects with others, he preferred other "solos" who would meet only when absolutely necessary and then disband as quickly as possible to head back to their respective solo caves.

As much as Don needed to share these insights with Joe and find out more about hierarchy and positioning, there was something else Joe had said that was eating at him. The suggestion Joe had made that Don had benched himself had struck a deep chord. Over the last few nights he'd even had dreams of being back on his high school baseball team, and they weren't pleasant dreams. In one dream, his team was losing, but Don couldn't get out of the dugout to take up his position at third base. As a result, run after run scored as the hitters learned to direct their hits to the hole at third base. Worst of all, in these dreams it wasn't at all clear whether Don couldn't or wouldn't step out onto the field. Don wasn't much for dream analysis or psychology, but he knew that there was something definitely going on there. He hoped Joe could help.

***

For a conceptual summary of this chapter, see page 107.

Chapter 2

POWER, AFFILIATION & ACHIEVEMENT

Although it was a bit difficult for Don to admit, he was beginning to understand that he had been placing everyone in the same category—his own—and then judging them for not doing things his way. This was especially problematic given that Joe had quite correctly helped him see that he wasn't even seeing himself clearly.

At Joe's request, Don met Joe in the clubhouse of a local private golf club. Also at Joe's request, he had done some homework before their meeting. When he arrived, he quickly spotted Dr. Joe at a table in the far corner.

"Thanks for meeting me here," Joe said as they shook hands.

"Thank you for fitting me in on such short notice," Don replied. "As I told you on the phone, our short conversation last week really had an impact."

Don quickly filled Joe in on his insight about grouping people into the three mammal categories, and on his baseball dreams. When he was finished, Joe nodded and asked him if he'd done his homework, saying that what he had in mind should clear some things up. Don got out four pieces of paper. On each one was the layout and description of the offices of Jack, Casey, their Boss, and himself. It had been a very interesting assignment, and Don was curious about Joe's intention.

"Are these actual photos of their desks?" Joe asked.

"Yes," Don replied. "You said to get a very detailed description of the desk, and so I figured a picture was worth a thousand words." Don was proud of the embedded desk photos on the PowerPoint printouts. Not only had he been forced to be a bit sneaky to get the desk photos, but he was pleased at how well the digital camera on his new super-smart phone had worked. He'd gotten the phone less than a month ago, and it came with every bell and whistle.

Joe laughed. "Jeez," he said, "I hope we don't get arrested for these. Were you followed here?"

They laughed together at Don's enthusiasm for completing Joe's homework assignment. Don felt a little embarrassed, but it also felt good to be excited about doing something. It was a feeling that he'd not had very often in the last year or so.

Joe explained that the reason he'd asked Don to observe the four offices in detail was that he expected that they would be useful for making sense of Don's insight about classifying people into the three mammal groups.

"As it turns out," Joe began, "your insight was right on, with some important tweaking needed." He then told Don about the work of David McClelland, the Harvard psychologist who had researched and written about social motivation. McClelland found that there are essentially three motivational styles: Power, Affiliation, and Achievement. While none of these motives comes in pure form, there is always a natural, preferred motivational expression that underlies a person's motives. However, these motives are mostly hidden agendas since they are more implicit than explicit, and knowing a person's preference will give you great leverage as you adapt your interactions to line up with his or her motivational worldview bias.

"So let me see," said Don, "As the solo animal I prefer Achievement, Jack is definitely all about Power and hierarchy, and Casey is Affiliation. She's good with teams and building relationships. But I'm not sure about the Boss."

"Not so fast," cautioned Joe. "Things may not be that simple." He explained how in a dynamic world, people may appear to change their preference from one situation to another. Also, the mammal groups are for classifying all mammals, and humans are definitely hierarchical. "Positioning, in other words, is a given," Joe stated. "It's just that we have different styles or ways of positioning. McClelland has shown us that we can identify the three basic motivational styles for positioning as Power, Affiliation, and Achievement."

"I get it," said Don. He prided himself on being a quick study. "People position themselves through Power, Affiliation, and Achievement. The mammal groups that are not hierarchical aren't really even positioning themselves. Maybe they don't even have that instinct."

"Exactly. And we must also keep in mind that we all contain a mixture or blend of these motivational styles," Joe added. "One is not inherently better than another. It's how we use them that counts." He then asked Don to chart his own mixture of McClelland's motives by taking 100 points and coming up with numbers for each.

Don came up with these numbers:

Power: 0
Affiliation: 10
Achievement: 90

"Wow, that's a lot of Achievement," Joe replied. "Let's go over each of the types to make sure you have a clear understanding of them."

Joe started with Power, and explained that people motivated by Power have a desire to exert their influence over others and situations. They often like things done their way, or want other people to follow their directions. Power motivations include a good reputation, status, and the ability to influence others by directing, supervising and controlling. Of course another Power motivation is competing against and even dominating others—and Power-motivated people are keenly aware of how they and others are maintaining or increasing position. Joe also made it a point to emphasize that true leaders understand and know how to use Power positively, and that leaders who take charge and make decisions are vital if an organization wants to make it. In other words, Joe emphasized, Power is a positive force in organizational excellence.

People motivated primarily by Affiliation, on the other hand, want to be associated with other people. They are keenly motivated by a social orientation. This means they like to participate as part of a team and like to work with people. They also have a need to be liked, which includes their need for acceptance and positive interpersonal relationships. In short, relationships are first, last and always. As a result, people motivated by Affiliation like to minimize conflicts and maximize harmony through cooperation and positive emotion. Joe made sure to point out that just like Power and Achievement, Affiliation is a necessary and very important motivation in the business world.

Lastly, Joe explained the motivational style of Achievement. People who are primarily interested in Achievement want a sense of personal accomplishment. They often seek out challenging and competitive situations, set realistic and achievable goals, and set a standard of personal excellence for themselves. Often they think about *how* things happen and have a tendency to be thing or idea oriented rather than people motivated. They are motivated to develop new and original ideas and applications, and to set long-range objectives. In business organizations, Joe emphasized, the motivation of Achievement can be the backbone of production. The downside of Achievement was a tendency to try and go it alone even when collaboration would be the wiser choice.

"Does this help?" Joe asked. He was watching Don's face throughout the explanation and thought he saw a few light bulbs go on.

"Definitely," said Don. He looked back at his original numbers. "I think I should adjust these a little," he said. As much as he identified with Achievement, he also heard important aspects of how he approached most situations contained in the description of Affiliation, as well as in Power.

"Let me give you a couple of real-world examples that may help," said Joe with a smile. "Ever see Star Trek?"

"Sure."

"Think of Kirk as Power, Bones as Affiliation, and Spock as Achievement."

Don smiled. He'd watched Star Trek a lot when he was younger, and he'd even purchased a Star Trek DVD a couple of years back. Thinking of Captain Kirk as Power helped him also to see Power in a more positive light.

"Or to be more up to date, you know American Idol?"

"Who doesn't?"

"Of the original three judges, which judge was which type?"

Don couldn't believe how obvious that now was. The three judges were clearly divided up into the three types: Paula was Affiliation, Simon was Power, and Randy was Achievement.

"Care to rethink your numbers?" Joe asked. "It seems to me you might have shortchanged yourself a little."

When Don thought it over more, he realized that he was motivated somewhat by Power, and he was also more motivated by Affiliation than he had first recognized. The new numbers Don came up with were:

Power: 20
Affiliation: 20
Achievement: 60

"That seems more like it," said Joe, uncovering a slip of paper where he had written 25, 25, and 50. " Your earlier numbers may actually represent how you usually feel because you are overcompensating in Achievement because you lack positioning and rapport skills."

"How do you mean?" Don asked. It felt a bit uncomfortable to be read by someone who could read you better than you were able to read yourself, but Don was curious and wanted to learn more.

Joe ticked several items off on his finger. "Senior management, former baseball player, able to easily approach a stranger in a café and quickly have a rather personal conversation. Shall I go on?" he asked.

Don sat silently for a moment. He was realizing that if he hadn't been seeing himself clearly, there might be a number of other important things he wasn't getting right.

"So what about the office photos?" he asked, in part to change the subject.

"Well, why don't you tell me what you see, in terms of Power, Affiliation and Achievement?" Joe suggested.

Don had already thought a little bit about the differences he saw, and now that he knew about Power, Affiliation and Achievement, he immediately noticed some things. For each photo and office description, he began to list for Joe what he thought fit in which motivational category. For the Boss's office it was easy. Biggest office with the best view—that was Power. A photograph with a former US President, that seemed to be Affiliation and Power. And the desk itself, a cherry antique that Don had long admired, seemed also to symbolize Power.

"Am I missing anything?" he asked Joe.

"You've got the gist of it," Joe replied, "but I wonder about the desk. A lot of antique collectors I know really value the story of how they acquired the antique at least as much if not more than its actual value. So it could be that this desk could represent Achievement."

"You're right," said Don, impressed. "I've actually heard him tell the story several times about how he spotted the desk at an estate auction, but it was painted over and superficially in bad shape. He bought it for almost nothing, then had it fixed up."

Joe nodded. "And look at how immaculate it is," he added. "That also denotes Power. What about the other offices?"

Don quickly went over Casey's office, which seemed much more inviting than the Boss's, and not only because it was smaller. Casey had a couple of chairs arranged so that impromptu meetings could be accommodated, and she also had an end table on which there was usually a neat stack of papers and books, many labeled with names. Don knew about this stack, for more than once Casey had taken something off of it and handed it to him. She was truly a wealth of information, he realized, and she was always looking to get just the right book or journal to help someone with a project or even a personal issue. All this networking, it seemed to Don, was Affiliation. Joe agreed, with one addition.

"What do you think she gets out of her networking?" he asked.

"She really cares about people," Don replied. "So I guess she gets the satisfaction of helping them out."

"And is that why you chose her to lead your core team?"

"No, I chose her because people really like working with her, and because she's so smart," Don answered. He'd rarely met anyone with a mind that worked as quickly as Casey's, and more than once her quick thinking had gotten their group out of a jam. Suddenly he recognized how he'd been underestimating her.

"And if I'm honest," he added, "I wanted her to run interference for me, to keep everyone a step or two away so that I could work without being interrupted so much."

"Would it be fair to say that she uses her Affiliation at least in part for Achievement and Power?" Joe asked.

"Absolutely. She knows so many people in the industry that sometimes just a quick phone call made to a former co-worker saves us days of work." This discussion was really making him see how much Casey contributed. He made a mental note to add this to her next performance review.

From there, Don assessed his own office and desk, down to the signed World Series baseball he'd caught when he was a freshman in college. There was also a picture of himself climbing the Flatirons in Colorado, and the gold-plated test tube he was awarded for the breakthrough that had first given him his reputation as a rising star. In addition, he had three working computers in the office, and a standard-issue desk that always had a sprawling stack pile of color-coded file folders for his work in progress. No photographs were there, except a small one on the bookshelf of his wife and son that was only visible to him when he was sitting at his desk.

"No Affiliation, and everything else appears to be Achievement," he concluded to Joe.

"Perhaps," Joe smiled. "What about that gold test tube?"

"Power?" Don questioned hesitatingly.

Joe nodded. "What was that you said about a rising star?"

Don laughed. He wasn't used to laughing these days, and it felt good. Calling Joe had definitely been a smart move.

They moved on to Jack's office, which Don had found quite interesting. For one thing, Jack's office furniture, though it was basically the same as Don's, looked in much better shape. There were also a couple of very artistic pieces of small sculpture on an end table, and a large vase-shaped pot containing a healthy, exotic-looking plant. "He reveals almost nothing personal about himself," Don announced suddenly. "That must be Power-motivated." To a large degree, he was using his other experiences of Jack to make that assessment, but it made sense to him.

"Perhaps not only," said Joe. "What's this little medallion on his desk?"

Don looked closely at the photograph and tried to recall it in his mind. It was round and bronze, about the size of a half-dollar, and it lay flat on the desk in a small frame. He'd not paid much attention to it when in Jack's office because it didn't seem important, but now he realized that it was the only personal thing on the desk. "Looks like some kind of medal," he said.

"Is Jack some kind of athlete?"

Don suddenly had the impression that he didn't know Jack very well at all, and this concerned him. He and Jack had been going head-to-head for a little over a year now, and Don felt all at once that he might be at a distinct disadvantage. Certainly the Boss's recent praise of Jack had made things seem that way.

"So what do you make of Jack?" he asked.

Joe agreed that Jack appeared from the looks of his office to be Power-motivated, but he cautioned about making too many hard and fast conclusions based on appearances. Often, he explained, it is better to look at what isn't being revealed, much like in Asian art where what is suggested is more important than what is stated. Joe also suggested that there were much better ways to find out about Jack's motivations.

"Like what?" Don asked.

"Just ask questions," said Joe. "But we'll get into that a bit later. Tell me first of all, what do you want to do with all this new knowledge? What's your goal here?"

Don rested his chin on his thumb in the thinker's pose, and stared out past Joe to the golf greens. Already what he had learned from knowing about Power, Affiliation and Achievement motivations was changing how he thought about what was going on in the office. For one thing, he recognized that he had not been paying enough attention to how everyone was operating, how their motivations were clearly different. Although it was a bit difficult for Don to admit, he was beginning to understand that he had been placing everyone in the same category—his own—and then judging them for not doing things his way. This was especially problematic given that Joe had quite correctly helped him see that he wasn't even seeing himself clearly.

"I want to learn how to use this information to do my job better," Don said after a few moments.

Joe smiled. "That we can do," he said. "How would you like to start?"

"With Casey," Don said. "I really see how I've not been noticing the contribution she makes."

"Okay, let's start by comparing her numbers to yours. How would you spread 100 points for her among Power, Affiliation and Achievement?"

Don wrote down his revised numbers, and then thought about Casey. Of course she seemed primarily Affiliation to him, but he also now realized that she used her networking and people skills for Achievement. As for Power, he wondered if her attitude wasn't a bit like his was, that is, seeing Power in a mostly negative light. In the end, these are the numbers he came up with:

<u>Don</u>   <u>Casey</u>
Power: 20   Power: 5
Affiliation: 20   Affiliation: 60
Achievement: 60   Achievement: 35

"Interesting," said Joe. "Why do you rank her so low in Power?"

Don explained that Casey seemed to have no interest in advancing her career. When he had first approached her about working for him, she had been a tough sell. She didn't want to leave the division she was working for—especially the people, it had seemed to him—even though it meant a lot more money and better advancement opportunities.

"How did you get her to change her mind?"

"I convinced her that we'd make a good team," Don replied.

"You played the Affiliation card. Nicely done," he said.

Joe then explained that since Affiliation-motivated people like to be part of a team, they find language that matches that motivation appealing. He then outlined words and phrases used by Affiliation-motivated people that could also be used to motivate them. They included:

- Let's get together
- Team effort
- Let's do something for...
- Group effort
- Togetherness
- Help others

He then detailed specific actions to take with an Affiliation-motivated person. These included:

- Reward contributions to the group
- Thank them for helping others get along and work together
- Recognize the importance of social interactions
- Smooth over potential conflicts

As Joe was going over this, Don's thoughts were going a mile a minute. He suddenly had a number of good ideas about how he would be able to better relate to Casey and make up for his past oversights. He also somehow felt confident that they would be able to work better together and clear up some of the problems he saw with how she was doing her job. But just as he was starting to feel really good, he stopped himself.

"Isn't this manipulation?" he asked. "I mean, aren't you just manipulating people when you find out their motivation type and then use that information to get them to do what you want?"

"Isn't that what you did when you convinced her that you two would make a good team together?"

"No," replied Don, "Because I didn't do it so calculatingly. What we're talking about here is 'politics,' which I hate." Don was surprised at how quickly he'd gotten worked up. His heart was racing, and he could feel his palms starting to sweat a little.

"Okay," said Joe. "Think about this. You're playing baseball, and your team picks up a new first baseman from another league, maybe in Japan. It's at the very end of the season, weeks away from the World Series. As the third baseman, you need to know all about how this guy plays first base, and you need to pick it up right away. You all want to win the Series. There's no time to learn intuitively through experience, and his English isn't so great so you can't even ask him much. Your infield coach hands you a scouting report on his fielding. Do you read it?"

"Of course," says Don.

"In the report, you read that he sometimes has trouble with balls thrown low and to his left. What do you do?"

"I make sure I throw high, maybe a bit to the right," Don answers, almost without thinking.

"So you use the information so that you can all win," Joe says matter-of-factly.

Even before Joe had finished his sentence, Don got it. This was not manipulation; this was simply using information that would help them both win. Casey's performance was likely to improve when Don applied his new understanding about motivation, and his own job performance would also improve when they were working together better. More than that, he suspected that applying his new understandings with others would deepen his own self-understanding.

"So what do you think?" Joe asked, "Is any of this helpful?"

It was Don's turn to smile. "Yes," he replied. "Very."

"How are you going to apply this to your problems with Casey?"

Don listed a number of things he was planning to do, starting with letting Casey know how much he recognized and appreciated her contributions. Some of the other ideas were still a bit rough, but he felt confident that with his greater understanding of the Affiliation motive he would be able to make things go much more smoothly—to their mutual benefit.

"Tell me," Joe asked, "Are you grooming Casey to take over for you if you take that promotion?"

It was a good question because it was something Don had given very little thought to. In fact, until meeting with Joe he had still been taking the attitude that he wasn't sure he even wanted the job. The memory of Joe's comment about "benching himself" returned, and Don suddenly felt more interested in beating out Jack for the promotion. Something of his old "rising star" fire had returned, and Don liked how it felt.

"I definitely need to keep that in mind," Don said. He felt that with some guidance Casey could do the job well, but he wasn't certain that she would even be interested. "And I should in any case prepare someone to take over because that improves my promotion potential," he added. "Of course I can still always say 'no' to the job once it's been offered, so I'm better off really putting myself in the running. I learned long ago that it's better to have options."

"Sounds good," said Joe. "Just one thing. Don't be so certain that Casey has as little Power motivation as you imagine. She could simply be satisfying her needs for Power in other ways. Observe her for a few days before you act on your new ideas about her."

Don nodded thoughtfully, then hurried out of the clubhouse to his car.

***

For a conceptual summary and this chapter's supplemental material, see page 108.

Chapter 3

COOPETITION® &
KING ARTHUR

He described this blend of competition and cooperation, which he called coopetition, as the essence of business positioning. Always positioning one's self as one-up or at least one-even was the hallmark of successful business people.

Over the next several days Don returned in his mind again and again to the conversation with Joe. It amazed him how much the information about Power, Affiliation and Achievement was changing how he did his job. People, he realized, were in one sense actually less complicated than he'd thought. He also realized that the more he paid attention to people and their motives, the more success he seemed to be having in getting things done.

What surprised Don most, however, was how much he had been misreading Casey. He had always known that she was extremely competent, which was why he'd wanted her to work for him in the first place, but now it was as if he were seeing her through new eyes. Joe had suggested that he simply observe her for a couple of days before charging ahead with one of his new ideas for working better with her, and he was glad he had followed this advice. Don quickly saw how Casey used her Affiliation motive for both Achievement and Power, so much so that he felt he was going to have to revise his 100-point distribution for her.

Don also realized that he had been wrong about Affiliation. Through his observation of Casey, together with Joe's clarification of motivational styles and strategies, he was forced to see that there was much more to it than he ever would have thought. Casey's ability to put people at ease and really listen to them, for example, helped her quickly pinpoint potential trouble and have her recommendations be accepted as positive suggestions and not criticism. He had to admit that his own Achievement motivation had become something of a bias for him, to the degree that his tendency had been to unconsciously downplay or even dismiss the workings of the other motivations—or even not to see them at all. Now that everything was up on the table, however, he was beginning to understand how all three motivations were integral, that they mutually complemented one another. He still wasn't sure if he had learned enough to directly confront Casey about the team's consistency problem, but he was going to do his best.

The opportunity came sooner than expected. The latest team project report had some glaring inconsistencies, and

Don needed to speak to Casey right away. He had been counting on this report to support his bid for a greater piece of the research budget, and he knew that Jack would hone right in on the weaknesses and try to derail him. Too much was at stake here for Don to be okay with the project report. Some of Jack's team had already been sniffing around for potential problems, and Don wasn't going to let them win this time. He scheduled an 8 a.m. meeting with Casey for the following day.

Casey, as always, arrived promptly. Don had told her that the meeting was about the project report, and her copy was in her hand as they sat down. Trying to apply his new knowledge of motivation, Don held back his inclination to get right to the point and spent a few minutes just talking with her. He then thanked her for how well she had handled a recent personnel change in the team and told her how much he admired her ability to work with people. As he spoke, Don watched as Casey literally seemed to light up.

"Thank you," she said, "These are really great people you've put together."

"Well, they certainly like and respect you," he replied. "And I think you really make things go extra smoothly around here." These were things Don had always noticed, but this was the first time he had complimented Casey directly on her Affiliation talents. His usual tendency was to stick to the numbers and offer feedback on her tactical strategies, which was something he now thought was probably about his own Achievement motive feedback needs.

"About the report," he continued. "I think we're going to have to redo a lot of it." He deliberately used "we" to highlight how this was a team effort, which was an Affiliation motivator.

Don then explained to Casey where he saw the inconsistencies, and he also clarified the importance of the report in terms of the current in-house budget war. In the past he probably would have left that part out, but since it was really a lot about people, it made sense to him to directly involve his people expert. As Joe had said, it was always all about Positioning, and Positioning was always all about people.

"The problems in the report are my personal responsibility," Casey said once she saw what Don was specifically referring to. "I'll get right on it."

"How can I help?" asked Don. It had occurred to him that he needed to be more involved in the team's work. "It's also my responsibility, so we should do this together."

They talked about how to best deal with the problem, and Casey suggested that they call everyone together and get it all straightened out as soon as possible. Don agreed, and told her that he would meet everyone in the conference room at 10.

After the meeting, Don felt great. He couldn't recall having had a better meeting with Casey. This was especially noteworthy since he had often in the past had difficulty giving feedback that could be seen as negative. In this case, by directly relating to Casey's Affiliation motive, he had managed to say what needed to be said without any bad vibes. What's more, he had also seen that the responsibility for the report's inconsistencies had equally been his. Had he stayed more in the loop with Casey they could have easily caught things much earlier. Affiliation, he had now experienced, was more important for achieving things than he might have guessed. High on his success, Don prepared for the 10 a.m. meeting, and looked forward to his next meeting with Joe. Although he knew there was more to learn about working with those high in Affiliation, he was also feeling ready to start working with Joe on how to deal with his Boss, ...and with Jack.

Joe and Don met the following day back at the Java Hut. Now that he had officially enlisted Joe to coach him, the coffee break was totally legit. In fact, he had told Casey where he was going, and that he had begun working with a performance coach. In their daily meeting, Don had almost told his Boss as well, but then thought better of it. For now he would play things a bit close to the vest until he'd had an opportunity to run things by Joe. After all, wasn't that the point of having a coach?

Since Joe and Don had already talked briefly on the phone about how things had gone with Casey, they jumped right into it.

"It sounds like things went really well with Casey," Joe commented. "I especially like how you tailored your approach to meet her Affiliation motivations. Did you learn anything unexpected from your experience with her?"

"Mostly that the Power, Affiliation and Achievement motives have been a huge blind spot for me," replied Don.

"Now that it's on your radar, what's next?"

Don had been thinking a lot about this. At the meeting with Casey and the core team, he had noticed how everyone was highly Achievement-motivated—including Casey, who used her primary Affiliation motivation as a means to Achievement. This made sense; after all, Don had put that team together to really produce, which for the most part they had. As for the consistency problems that they were experiencing, Don discovered that they were largely due to a kind of turf war going on between two of the team members. Casey had actually been doing a great job of keeping the ball rolling given the circumstances, but Don could see that below the thin surface of collegiality there was a real storm brewing. These two guys seemed like oil and vinegar, and were ready to go at each other at the drop of the hat. Don gave Joe the overview, and asked for his take on things.

"How do they stack up on Power, Affiliation and Achievement?" asked Joe immediately.

While Don had thought about their motives, he hadn't actually done their 100-point numbers. He did so now on a Java Hut napkin, explaining as he did them that this was just a best guess.

	Chris	Raj
Power	40	30
Affiliation	10	00
Achievement	50	70

"So what are you saying with those numbers?" Joe wanted to know.

"Well," said Don, "When I think about it, it's surprising how alike they are. My impression, though, is that Chris is somewhat more motivated by Power and Affiliation, and Raj is much more Achievement—so much so that he doesn't seem to have any idea of the importance and necessity of Affiliation." This last bit, Don realized as he spoke, was an insight he had gained from his recent interaction with Casey.

Joe explained that as much as this numbers exercise was probably just an approximate measure, it did offer an opportunity to really sit down and think about a person's motives. He added that a point difference of 20 or more — as existed here in Achievement—often pointed to potential conflict, depending of course on the rapport and positioning skills of the parties in question. In this case, he believed that there were several possible explanations for the turf warfare.

"How do they generally position themselves in relation to one another?" he asked Don.

Don wasn't quite sure how to answer. "What do you mean?" he asked.

Joe took out his notepad and drew the same diagram he had drawn for Don the first time they met. This time, however, he added more. Then he explained that there is only one of four possible positions that anyone can occupy in any given situation, as demonstrated by King Arthur's court:

- One-up: King Arthur is one-up on everyone in the kingdom.
- One-down: The knights are one-down to the king.
- One-even: The knights are one-even to each other (they all have the same rank).
- One-apart: Merlin the Magician is one-apart—off to the side, though indirectly part of the system.

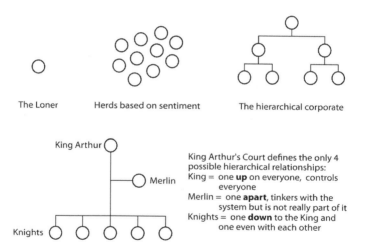

The Loner   Herds based on sentiment   The hierarchical corporate

King Arthur's Court defines the only 4 possible hierarchical relationships:
King = one **up** on everyone, controls everyone
Merlin = one **apart**, tinkers with the system but is not really part of it
Knights = one **down** to the King and one even with each other

"In other words," Joe said, "Like everyone, these two are competitively positioning themselves, but if they're negatively affecting the productivity of the team, then they have some misunderstandings about their roles. They are seeing themselves as solo players, not as team members who are one-even in the context of the team. The question is: what are you going to do about it?"

"Because I'm King Arthur here, right?" replied Don.

Joe nodded.

"I think it's fair to say that I've been trying to play Merlin," Don said with a smile. Increasingly it was becoming clear to him that he had been relying too much on Casey to handle the people side of things because he hadn't had the knowledge or skills to do so himself. In fact, he used to feel that it wasn't really his job to deal with any interpersonal conflicts, and he had gone out of his way to create an environment that shielded him from such things.

"So how do I take charge here?" he asked.

"Let's think baseball," said Joe. "How do players compete?"

"As a team," Don replied automatically.

"But don't they compete individually as well? Like for the highest batting average on the team or the fewest errors made? And aren't they also competing for the fans' attention, and for the best salary deal?" Joe asked.

"Sure."

"So being on a team is a blend of competition and cooperation?"

"Of course."

"It's no different in business," Joe explained. He described this blend of competition and cooperation, which he called coopetition, as the essence of business positioning. Always positioning one's self as one-up or at least one-even was the hallmark of successful business people.

"But Chris and Raj are positioning themselves as one-up, and they're causing problems," Don pointed out.

"What they're doing would be like the second baseman trying to cover the shortstop position because he wants to show the shortstop up," said Joe. "Of course that leaves a big hole at second base where the competition can just hit grounders all day long."

Don got it. It was perfectly okay to play one-up in the appropriate areas of the game, but if the players don't cooperate then no one wins. He also saw that in the case of Chris and Raj, he was the coach, and that it was up to him to straighten them out. But he still wasn't quite sure how.

"So is that what I should explain to them?" he asked.

"You certainly could," Joe said. "But not so fast. If cooperation is the name of the team game, then where can they apply their motivation to compete?"

"In being the most cooperative," stated Don with conviction. "They could compete for doing the most for the team, which means knowing what position each team member is playing. And then they should deliver what they're responsible for while making it easy for the others to play their own positions." Perhaps for the first time, he understood that this is what great players do. They contribute to the team by developing and expressing their individual skills and talents in a cooperative way.

"Don't baseball players also pay very close attention to their personal stats?" Joe asked.

"That's true. Baseball is a game of statistics. So Chris and Raj can also compete against themselves, against their own performance standards," added Don.

"Yes," said Joe, feeding Don's insights. "We could even say that in one way these performance standards represent their personal brand, their business identity as a player. So they can develop this personal brand, and then sell it to you, because as their boss you are their customer."

Joe waited a moment for everything to sink in.

Don sat there, and when he took a sip from his cup he noticed that his coffee had cooled. He asked Joe if he wanted more hot water for his tea, then went up to the counter.

This also gave him some time to mull things over. When he returned, Joe got right back into things.

"Does all this make sense to you?" he asked.

Don smiled and nodded. Joe had a way of working his brain that he'd never experienced before, and he liked it. Their session had just started, and already he was seeing things in a new, practical way. Even though he'd heard it before, the concept that as their boss he was Chris and Raj's customer was a way of looking at the boss/employee relationship that he'd never given real weight to. But it made perfect sense. In fact, he saw that it was the only way for things to make sense. He had also never had anyone so clearly explain before how blending the apparent opposites of cooperation and competition were how business truly functions. Maintaining advantageous position, he realized now, was about knowing when, how and where to compete—and when, how and where to cooperate.

"So what Casey and I need to do," he said, "Is completely re-clarify the roles of the team members to themselves and everyone else. That will be step one. Then I need to have a one-on-one with Chris and with Raj."

"Shouldn't you include Casey?"

"Yes, Casey and I will meet individually with them and explain how we are their customers, and that we need them to supply us with what we want and how we want it, or we will find a new vendor!"

"And what about their personal conflict?" Joe asked.

Don thought about it for a moment. He then explained these two were good workers. Chris had been with him from almost the beginning at BioWidgets, and Raj was a real expert in his field. Their specialty areas did overlap some, just like a shortstop and second baseman, but that could be used to the team's advantage. The fact that they were fighting suggested that they saw each other as competitors... and not teammates. The truth, as Joe had pointed out with his coopetition concept, was that they were both. Once they understood that, any so-called personal issues they had with each other would probably go away. And if not, he told Joe, they would have to be professionals and not take it with them onto the playing field.

"What does all this say about Power and being a leader?" asked Joe once Don had finished speaking.

"A real leader knows the game is played by cooperating and competing," Don replied. "And it's my role to keep the roles clear so that the system works."

"Does all this apply to you and your Boss also?" Joe questioned.

"Yes," Don answered tentatively. He knew Joe well enough by now to understand that Joe's questions followed a direct line to the issue at hand, but he wasn't sure where this was going.

"How well are you two getting along?"

In previous conversations Don had told Joe of his troubles with his Boss. Mostly, he felt that his Boss favored Jack and Jack's input over his own, but for no discernible reason. Don believed that he was the one who consistently had the better ideas, and the track record to prove it. He was also much more experienced in the lab than Jack, and he worked harder and more hours than Jack. Not only that, but Jack had a way of turning Don's ideas into his own and then presenting them to the Boss that way. Don had learned the hard way to be more guarded around Jack, but things still had not improved. Lately in fact the situation had gotten worse as the immanent merger had raised the stakes. There was going to be a new research division created, and Don and Jack appeared to be the frontrunners for the job. For a while Don had lost his taste for the new job, but now his work with Joe had given him a new perspective—and had relit his fire. Somehow, with Joe's help, he needed to let his Boss see that he, not Jack, was the better choice.

Don explained to Joe the most recent happenings, which included the upcoming budget fight that he was preparing for with Casey and the team's report.

"We're getting along well enough," he said, "but I am noticing that the Boss continues to see me in the way Jack has manipulated things."

"What way is that?" asked Joe.

"Well, after Jack basically stole my idea for the nano-enzymes, the Boss looks at me as a has-been or something. I spent a lot of time developing those models and doing the preliminary essays, and now I'm having to play second fiddle to Jack—who really doesn't know what he's doing and keeps using me and my team to bail him out of jams we wouldn't have gotten into in the first place."

"So he's cast you as one-down, is that what you're saying?"

"That's right," he replied. Stated so bluntly, it seemed almost too simple to Don. But that was exactly what had happened.

"Doesn't this sound familiar?" Joe asked. "A turf war?"

Don might have laughed at this strange coincidence if it weren't so serious. Chris and Raj were having their positioning conflict just like he and Jack were having theirs, but in this case he was in the opposite position. And so far, it seemed like the Boss had been handling it by letting them fight it out. Of course Jack and he weren't on the same team in the way that Chris and Raj were, and that had allowed Jack to get away with a lot of what Don thought of as political nonsense.

"Before we get into things with Jack, let's look at your relationship with your Boss," suggested Joe. "What can you tell me about him in regard to Power, Affiliation and Achievement?"

Don wrote out what he thought were the Boss's numbers, and then placed them alongside his own.

	Boss	Don
Power	40	20
Affiliation	20	20
Achievement	40	60

"What does this tell you?"

Using Joe's 20 point rule-of-thumb, Don interpreted the numbers to mean that there was potential for conflict for Don and his Boss in both Power and Achievement.

"Let's start by looking at the Achievement motivation, which is your strongest motivation." Joe then explained again how a person primarily motivated by Achievement wants a sense of personal accomplishment. He also explained some Achievement motivations:

- Competing against a challenge or standard more than against others
- Setting high standards of achievement/accomplishment
- Developing new and original ideas and applications
- Setting long-range objectives
- Planning for contingencies

Next, Joe went over the actions one could take to appeal to an Achievement-motivated person:

- Recognize their achievement through words and/ or awards
- Encourage initiative

- Encourage independent thinking
- Have them participate in seeking goals and planning target dates
- Demonstrate appreciation for accuracy and planning
- Keep projects interesting and challenging

Don definitely saw himself in the Achievement motivations, and he also recognized that he was motivated by the actions for appealing to an Achievement-motivated person. In fact, he quickly identified a couple of reasons why he had lost such interest in his job recently and had felt rather lukewarm about the possible promotion. Over the past year—approximately since Jack had come onto the scene, his Boss had included him less and less in what Joe had called goal seeking. In addition, Don felt that the value of his work was not being recognized, which bothered him more than anything else. He explained both of these things to Joe.

"Does any of this sound familiar?" asked Joe.

"What do you mean?"

"Do you think Casey might have had any of these feelings?"

Don was quiet. Joe had again pointed out the elusive obvious; what he was experiencing seemed to be the mirror image of what he had helped create for Casey by not recognizing and knowing how to handle her Affiliation motivations. She had no doubt felt that she was not being appreciated for her contributions, and since Don had to some degree left her out of the loop on some of his job's larger issues, such as the details of the ongoing budget war, she might have felt that she and he weren't really working together. Don was truly surprised at how neatly this all fit together. He never would have believed that his blind spots concerning the motives of Power, Affiliation and Achievement could create such trouble for himself and for others.

"I get it," said Don. "What I don't see affects both what I let happen to me—as well as what I do to others."

"That's right. Let's look at Power now," said Joe. "Then we can have the full 360 degree view."

Joe reviewed how people highly motivated by Power often are seen negatively in our culture and are frequently viewed suspiciously. The truth, he explained, is that a person with a high need for the positive use of Power is a valuable asset in the managerial structure of any thriving organization. This is because organizational structure involves relationships among people who are constantly influencing one another and positioning themselves. If the organization is to survive, let alone thrive, some people must assume positions of management and concern themselves with the exercise of Power that makes it possible to achieve the goals of the organization.

Effective business leaders, Joe explained further, are characterized by a high need for this positive type of Power. They formulate clear, persuasive goals, and inspire others to achieve these goals. They make subordinates feel strong,

capable, and effective...like initiators rather than blind fol-
lowers. They have a concern for finding out and articulating
group goals in a manner that will motivate people, often
helping the group members to formulate the goals, and
then taking the first step in providing members with ways in
which they can attain these objectives. Most importantly, this
type of leader will inspire group members, giving them the
feelings of strength and competence they need to work hard
for their goals.

As Joe was speaking, Don couldn't help but think about his
Boss, and about Jack. Both clearly had high Power motivations, but he also saw differences in how they used Power.
With the Boss, for example, Don rarely felt that he was being
told what to do in an authoritarian way. Rather, the Boss
always seemed driven to find the most effective and efficient
plan of action, and he would take lots of time to make sure
that was found. Once a course was decided upon, however,
there was no turning back on an all-out forward march. Jack,
on the other hand, seemed less skillful than Don in his use of
Power, and at times Don had the impression that Jack made
decisions simply to assert his authority—even if he really
didn't have it.

Like with the other motives, Joe explained what generally
motivated those with a high drive for Power. He also gave
Don some sheets with the motivations for all three listed. For
Power it said:

- Good reputation or position
- Status

- Ability to influence others
- Directing, Supervising and Controlling
- Competing against or even dominating others

He then suggested actions to take with Power-motivated people:

- Acknowledge their status, position or authority
- Ask for their advice
- Give them credit for what they do
- Include them in meetings
- Recognize them publicly
- Give them authority to act
- Let them know they have influenced you
- Be supportive of their position even when critiquing performance
- Convince them that doing what you want will get them what they want
- Keep them up-to-date on all developments
- Provide symbols of authority

"How does this outline show how I should relate to my Boss?" asked Don. For the most part, he felt he was getting a better picture of things, but none of that had yet translated into real results. He had little time to turn things around before the Bosses decided on the new division leader, so he was eager to learn what Joe had to offer.

"Well, what do Chris and Raj have to do so that they better relate to you, Casey and the team?" Joe asked.

"They have to begin seeing themselves as their bosses' customers," answered Don. He recognized that this one simple concept had completely reshaped how he saw himself as a boss, and now as a subordinate. "So it appears that's what I should also do," he added.

Joe nodded. "Have you ever asked your Boss how you can better deliver the goods and services he needs?"

Don hesitated. "Isn't that up to him to tell me?" he asked.

Joe shrugged his shoulders. "What would asking him do for him, and for you?"

Don looked over the sheets Joe had given him on Power, Affiliation and Achievement. He thought of his Boss as both Achievement and Power, and tried to see what Joe was getting at.

"Well," he said. "Asking him would appeal to his position of authority, which is a Power motivator, and it would also appeal to his Achievement motivation by demonstrating that I am focused on helping him get his job done."

"And what would it do for you?"

Don thought the question over. It was true that he often assumed he knew what the Boss needed, and it was also true that sometimes there appeared to be a real gap between what he delivered and what the Boss liked. Occasionally he was even extremely surprised when the Boss rejected a project idea that Don had been certain was right on the money. Jack, on the other hand, seemed to have the Midas touch. Practically whatever he proposed, the Boss went for. It was even possible, Don mused, that the nano-enzyme project that Jack had taken from him and presented would have been one of those projects that the Boss dismissed had Don been the presenter. Clearly, Don realized, there was something in his delivery that wasn't matching up with what the Boss wanted.

"I think being clearer about what exactly the Boss is looking for could really improve my batting average," Don answered. "Especially now that I need to make up on some lost advantage."

"What do you mean?" Joe asked.

Don explained that before Jack had come along, he'd felt like he was the golden boy, the go-to guy the Boss relied on. And they had had some real successes together. When Jack had moved in from Corporate West, however, all that had changed. For a while, Don had assumed that the problem was what his wife called the "imported cheese syndrome," which meant that imported products were often perceived to be better even when they were not, and that Jack's luster would fade once the Boss got used to him. But now, Don had to accept that there was more to it than that.

"It sounds a little like you let him come in and set up shop on your front yard," said Joe.

"Yes," said Don. "I guess I thought I would just wait it out—and I didn't compete. Or better said, I stopped positioning myself."

"Did Jack do the same for you?" Joe asked.

"Not at all. Jack came in claiming turf from day one."

Don was amazed at how blind he had been. Jack had come in with a plan, and he had been implementing it every day since his arrival. His plan had been to become the new division leader. In fact, Don realized, Jack had no doubt known of the upcoming merger long in advance, but probably not much earlier than Don had found out about it. The difference was that Jack had formulated a strategy for working it to his advantage. That was why he had brought in most of his team with him—he wanted to hit the ground running. In addition, he'd probably promised them all promotions once he'd staged his coup. Don suddenly felt very foolish. He'd been complaining that Jack was power-hungry and playing politics when the truth was that Jack was just playing the game of business, and playing it very well.

***

For a conceptual summary, charts, and this chapter's supplemental material, see page 110.

Chapter 4

YOUR BOSS IS YOUR
CUSTOMER

"Actually, I'm here to ask you if there's anything I can do for you," Don said. "I know there's a lot going on right now, so I'd like to know how I can best help you get things done."

Over the next week, Don had many opportunities to apply what he was learning from Joe. Above all, competition with Jack was now on the front burner, and that was having some interesting effects. For one thing, Don and Casey were working better than ever as a team, and together they were successfully turning Chris and Raj around. Proof of this had come at the weekly group meeting when they had spontaneously agreed to take on a small project together—and seemed pleased to do so. Casey had smiled at Don as the two former antagonists were excitedly talking out the details, and after the meeting they two of them had a chance to talk about this latest development.

"Thank you so much for ironing everything out between Chris and Raj," Casey said as soon as they had sat down for their post-meeting review in Don's office.

"We did it together," Don said, "and I'm surprised at how easy it was. I think we've really helped them understand that if we work together, we win together. And most importantly, you have been great at showing them what real teamwork is. You've really modeled that well."

Casey nodded. "Thank you," she said. "I've sure tried. But what was it you told them a couple of days ago? That's what I saw make the biggest difference in how they relate to each other. It was immediately noticeable."

Don looked up from some papers he had just started looking through. "Really?"

Absolutely. I've never seen Chris so motivated, and Raj was actually smiling yesterday."

It continued to amaze Don, now that he knew more about Power, Affiliation and Achievement, how there were so many Affiliation type things that he just never saw but Casey picked right up on. He thought his follow-up meetings with Chris and Raj had gone well, yet he'd noticed nothing different about them until what he had just seen in the team meeting. He made a mental note to himself about making a conscious effort to be more alert to Affiliation.

"What I told them was basically the same thing, adjusted slightly for their different roles. I thanked them first of all for their excellent work, and then I reminded them of the benefits of truly being team players—that we would all win. I also reiterated what we expect from them in their individual roles, and reminded them that we are their customers, and that they must therefore supply us with what we need."

"And what did you tell them about the nano-enzyme project?" Casey asked. It had come out in their meetings with Chris and Raj that they were disappointed that the lead on the project had been taken from them and given to Jack's team.

"I told them that I had every intention for us to get the project back, and that I needed their best work to help make that happen."

"Wow," Casey remarked. "That must have been what motivated them."

Don smiled, and then reminded her that they still had a long way to go to beat out Jack and his team. Understanding the game that Jack was playing had completely shifted Don into high performance mode. Once that light about Jack's game plan had gone on, he'd called Casey in for a private meeting to strategize. She had revealed then that Jack had been hinting to her that she might want to switch teams, and when Don heard that he got the real wake-up call. He now knew that his assessment about Jack was dead-on. He also knew that if he didn't turn things around quickly, Jack was indeed going to open shop on Don's front lawn, as Joe had phrased it.

Don and Casey's strategy was simple. The first thing was to do what Jack had already done by coming in with a cohesive, dedicated team. In other words, they had to get their core team truly operating like a core team. No more playing second fiddle to Jack's team and doing mop-up tasks. Then they had to take the lead by getting the nano-enzyme project back. They were the ones who had the research and experience anyway. Now they just needed the leadership, and that was largely up to Don. As Joe had said, he had to be the leader, not the lead worker. Don was nervous, but he was also more excited than he had been in years. He started to feel at work what he used to feel as he stepped on to the baseball diamond: a mixture of confidence, daring and determination. Losing was not an option. There was no plan B, no safety net, because he knew that hedging his bets would allow Jack, who was clearly starting to pull out all the stops, to walk all over him. He explained to Casey that Jack's play for her was as much to destroy their team as it was for her talents and connections. That bold power move ended up having the opposite effect. Casey was a committed team player, and when Don pointed out that part of Jack's intent was to cripple their team, she appeared genuinely resolved not to allow that to happen.

For the rest of their meeting, Don and Casey continued working out their strategy to get the nano-enzyme project back. They had already instructed the team that open-door cooperation with Jack's team was over. Any request for assistance, even the borrowing of a book or beaker, was to be cleared by Casey. They needed to walk a fine line between corporate cooperation and team competition, and Don wanted to make sure that Jack was not given any more gems. He pointed out to Casey that if they knew where Jack's team was looking for help, they could get a sense of where there might be an advantage to be played.

The next day, Don attended their division's weekly meeting with the Boss, Jack, and the others. Up until recently they had met on Tuesdays, but Jack had somehow sold the Boss on changing the day to Thursday. This in itself was remarkable because the Boss had instituted standing weekly meetings as one of his first changes when he'd taken over the position five years earlier, and the day of the meeting had not changed in all that time. Considering everything else he was now seeing about Jack, on his way down the hall to the conference room Don considered the possibility that Jack's rationale for this schedule change was to gain advantage for himself and his group. Jack knew, for example, that Don's group still met on Wednesdays despite the division meeting day change, as did most other groups, and the consequence was that the agenda for the Wednesday meeting was sometimes now quickly made at least partially obsolete by what happened at Thursday's meeting. Don wondered if he were getting a bit paranoid, but whatever the truth of the matter was, he decided to change their group meeting to follow the divisional meeting so that they could be more efficient and effective with their time. He knew that Jack's group met on Fridays, which was good timing, but Don wanted to go one better and decided that from then on his group would meet immediately following the Thursday divisional meeting—starting immediately. After sitting down in the conference room, he pulled out his new phone and emailed Casey to that effect so that she could spread the word and get something set up for that very afternoon.

As he prepared his notes, Don reminded himself that he had made it his goal for the meeting to closely observe Jack and the Boss to see if he could learn anything that could help him in any way. He wasn't quite sure what he was looking for, but Joe had stressed many times that everything is always in the language, so Don was going to listen closely.

"Language is behavior," Joe had said at their last session. "Whenever people talk, their language reveals their motivation—both conscious and unconscious."

Don realized that he wouldn't be able to recognize most of what Joe was able to pick up on, but now that he had a basic understanding of Power, Affiliation and Achievement, he felt confident that he'd at least be able to recognize those patterns and strategies. And right from the start, Don witnessed something very interesting. For some reason, the Boss was late for the meeting, which was highly unusual, and Don overheard Jack talking to Vickie, the group leader who had been instrumental in getting Jack hired.

"If the Boss isn't here in a couple of minutes, I'm going to go ahead and introduce my presentation to get everyone up to speed," Jack said to her, apparently not concerned that he may be overheard. "That way when the meeting starts we'll be able to hit the ground running."

Don felt that in the past he would have interpreted such a comment at face value, in regard to his primary Achievement motivation at least. It was definitely true that getting the meeting going would save time, and he might have gone along with it on those grounds. What he heard now, however, was that Jack was acting from his motivation for Power. He was going to take control of the meeting and do things his way. The problem, as Don saw it, was that Jack was in a room of peers, not reports. And who knew what the Boss had planned? The Boss's assistant had informed them of a slight delay, and if the Boss had wanted them to start his assistant would have made that clear.

Without being obvious, Don watched Jack. He no longer felt at all threatened by him. Instead, Don's interest was now a kind of fascination. He thought that if he could learn to understand how Jack operated, he would learn more about the dynamics of Power, Affiliation and Achievement, as well as a lot about leadership. Jack, Don knew, was an excellent group leader, and he fully respected him for that. From what Don had seen, Jack really had the ability to manage and inspire his reports so that they did their best. Where Don felt Jack was deficient was in the details, the science of their business. But Jack had what seemed to be a great intuitive feel for when and how to move, and his team was hardworking, loyal and dedicated. Inspired by what he had already learned from Joe, Don realized that he had so much more to learn about people and business, and he saw his rivalry with

Jack as a perfect opportunity. Just as Jack was handing out notes for his presentation, the Boss arrived. Don watched as the Boss quickly sized up the situation and spoke.

"Once again, please excuse my tardiness," he said. "There are some exciting developments to share with you about the merger." He picked up the notes Jack had left for him and placed them to the side without saying anything.

The Boss then explained to them the latest on the merger with XYZygote, the genome research firm involved in the merger. The merger was finally being publicly announced that day, which meant that they could now speak openly of it. As the Boss explained the details of these developments, Don paid close attention to his language, hoping to find elements of Power, Affiliation and Achievement motivation. As expected, the Boss was appealing to their Achievement motivation by emphasizing what a fabulous opportunity this was going to be, full of exciting, groundbreaking projects. In doing so Don noted that he liberally used the words "goals," "hard work" and "innovation." Don also noted that most sentences contained the word "we," which clearly appealed to their Affiliation motivation. Surprisingly, Don detected little use of Power words, except for when the Boss spoke of the need they were going to have for true leadership throughout the merger and that there were going to be some opportunities for advancement and promotion, as well as some personnel cuts.

Immediately after the meeting, Don waited around for a few minutes while Jack talked to the Boss about the highlights of his presentation, for which there had been no time. When he finally caught the Boss's eye, Don asked him if he had time for a quick word in private. Don could feel Jack's eyes on him as he and the Boss agreed to meet in five minutes time at the Boss's office, and Jack continued looking at him after the Boss had walked out of the conference room.

"Exciting news about the merger," Don said, in an attempt at amicable small talk. "I'm especially looking forward to those promised new labs."

"Yes," Jack said, "I am as well. But let's see how long it takes to really get us up and running. The last merger I went through was quite painful."

They spoke a few more minutes about what they should and should not expect now that the merger was public knowledge, and Don was pleasantly surprised at how open and forthcoming Jack was being. This was the longest one-on-one conversation they'd had outside of a meeting in quite a while, and Don remembered why he had enthusiastically supported Jack's candidacy for his current position. Jack was a very likeable, engaging conversationalist, and he came across as sincere and warm. Somehow Don was a little surprised by how well they were getting along, given the circumstances. As Don left for the Boss's office, Jack joked about the Boss and Don carving up XYZygote for themselves, and Don promised to cut Jack in for a price.

When he arrived, the Boss was waiting for him.

"Sit down," he said warmly. "What's on your mind?"

Don had rehearsed this to himself all day long, and the words flowed easily.

"Actually, I'm here to ask you if there's anything I can do for you," Don said. "I know there's a lot going on right now, so I'd like to know how I can best help you get things done."

For the briefest of moments the Boss paused, and Don caught a flash of what seemed like surprise on his face.

"Thank you," he replied. "There is a tremendous amount of work to be done—both short and long term—and I'm just now starting to sort it out somewhat. Was there anything in particular you'd like to help with?"

Joe had helped Don anticipate this question, and he had a reply ready.

"I have some ideas, but first, what do you think is your best use of me, or me and my group?"

The Boss sat back in his chair and smiled.

"If only everyone were so agreeable," he said. He then proceeded to enlist Don's help in assessing XYZygote personnel on the middle and upper management levels. He wanted Don's take on who would fit in best where, and he wanted him to pull no punches. There were also a few current XYZygote projects in the works that he would like Don's team to check into, and he gave Don some names and phone numbers. By the time they were finished talking, nearly an hour had passed, and the Boss's assistant arrived at the door to take lunch orders for a meeting with a few key 'Zygote people due to arrive shortly. The Boss invited Don to stay, and Don made a quick call to Casey to check the status of their group meeting that afternoon. Things, he thought to himself as he hung up the phone, were going better than he ever could have planned.

***

For a summary of this chapter and supplemental material, see page 115.

Chapter 5

BUSINESS IS ALL ABOUT PEOPLE

In the past, Don would have been tempted to define positioning as "politics," but Joe had helped him realize that positioning is a given drive of human nature, and to ignore it was not noble or high-minded. Rather, choosing to ignore positioning was a common form of ignorance—one that Don had succumbed to.

Don's next meeting with Joe was back at the golf clubhouse. They had had some email and phone contact, so Joe was generally up to speed on the new developments in Don's career. Even so, he started the session by asking for an update.

"So what's the story these days?" Joe wanted to know. "Sounds like you're making things happen."

"More than I ever would have thought possible," Don replied. "It's overwhelming at times."

Joe laughed. "Are you the same guy I met hiding out in the coffee shop?" he asked.

"Sometimes I wonder," laughed Don. He then thanked Joe for how much he had been helping him. "I haven't enjoyed my job this much in years, maybe ever," he added.

"What would you like to accomplish in this meeting?"

Don thought for a second.

"I'd like to know how I can beat Jack out for the division leader position," he said. "I know I could do a better job."

"What makes you say that?"

"I know our company better, I do better research, and I always come in on budget."

"How do you know the company better?" Joe asked.

"I've been there longer and have been involved with countless projects and many people. So I have a good sense for where BioWidgets can go."

"How is all that going to be helpful in the merger?"

"Since we are more or less acquiring them, they are going to be adapting primarily to our culture rather than the other way around."

"And what does that mean?" asked Joe.

"It means that I am the better candidate for the job," Don replied quickly. "Jack knows BioWidgets West, but we do things differently."

"How?"

Don paused. "I'm not sure how to phrase it," he said. "We're just a little less flashy, and more prudent in what we get involved in. There are a lot of sketchy projects in this field, and we're definitely more conservative that way."

"How does that stack up against what Jack has to offer?" Joe asked.

"Jack is high caliber, no doubt about it," Don said. "And the reason we're the top candidates is that we are both BioWidgets players, and the Boss has said that they want someone from the inside for this one."

"And so how do you compare head to head with Jack?" asked Joe, repeating the question.

"On paper, I think we balance out pretty well," said Don. "We've both had some real successes, and our groups have consistently been the top performers over the last year. Where we differ is in our management styles, and maybe in our research interests. I'm not interested in pursuing something unless there's really been enough science there to warrant it. In fact that's what 'Zygote is bringing to the table. They have the people and labs to do preliminary research."

"Will that favor you or Jack?"

Don paused for a moment to consider.

"Actually," he said. "That should still favor me. I think Jack will take it as an opportunity to do even riskier research."

"And how do you think your management styles differ?"

"You ask a lot of questions," said Don with a half smile. "But it's good. Let's see. In your terms, I've been more of a Merlin—one-apart, and Jack is a King Arthur who likes to play one-up. But I can see that I am changing. Understanding Power, Affiliation and Achievement allows me to speak to the team in ways that will actually motivate them and build rapport."

Joe smiled. "It sounds to me like you have a solid case to build for yourself," he said. "And from what you've told me, you've made some real progress in your relationship with your boss."

Don nodded. "That was a real coup the other day when he invited me to stay for the lunch meeting with the 'Zygote people."

"What about your brand?" Joe asked. "Do you remember before when we talked about how individual baseball players create a business identity based on their performance standards? In the coming weeks it would be a good idea for you to continue building your brand."

"What do you suggest?"

Joe explained that there are three aspects to every business: finance, technology and people. However, since people are the ones who make the decisions in finance and technology, in the end, business is really all about people. Joe also remarked that almost everything Don had said about his competitive advantage over Jack was people-related: for example that he knew more people than Jack in the organization, and that he understood the BioWidgets-East culture better, which would be a definite advantage in the merger. The other positive point of comparison, his technological advantage, would also play a significant role in his personal brand.

"Branding is all about positioning," Joe added. "We have to position your bid for the job in such a way that your Boss sees how it is to his advantage to promote you over Jack. For example, your brand could be: A leader and proven research pro who knows the BioWidgets people and culture."

"I like it," said Don. "And it differentiates me from Jack."

"How so?" Joe asked. "What would you say Jack's brand is at this point?"

Don thought for a minute. "Jack has positioned himself as a leader—a dynamic leader," he said. "One who likes to push the edge."

"A dynamic leader and innovator?" suggested Joe.

"Exactly."

"But is that what BioWidgets needs for this position?"

"No," Don said. "I really think we need to utilize what this merger will bring, and we can only do that if we first build our new team up."

"Sounds like a sound byte," said Joe. "Use it."

Don felt good, and his confidence was building as they spoke.

"So how do I do that?" he asked.

"Who needs to hear it?"

"The Boss."

"Then tell him," Joe said. "You have the product he needs, and he'll want to know that. It's your job to deliver what he needs, which could mean having to tell him exactly what you offer."

There it was again. Don was struck by how reactive he was used to being with the Boss. Rather than seeing his Boss as his customer, in many ways he was in the habit of expecting the Boss to tell him what he wanted and what to do. Don spoke up at meetings and offered his thoughts and advice there, but that was more or less where it stopped. His recent request to speak privately with the Boss had been an exception, and Don realized now how that direct, proactive action had opened some doors for him. He was ready for more.

"And what about Jack?" Don asked.

"What about him?"

"How do I compete with him?"

"Establish your brand, and don't let him corner any markets," said Joe. "Marketing 101." Don immediately thought of the nano-enzyme project, and told Joe of his and Casey's plan to get it back somehow. Don realized as he was speaking that if they were able to pull that off that the position would have to go to him. In fact, he finally understood now why Jack had been so keen to muscle in on his territory in the first place—and even felt a bit foolish that he had not thought of it before. It was a perfect merger project that would highlight how XYZygote and BioWidgets could work together. In addition, getting the project back in his group's hands would show that Don could play hardball when necessary. The trick was to do it in a way that showed leadership and innovation, which was Jack's so-called territory.

Once again, Don was struck by the change he had gone through. It was even difficult for him to imagine how he used to think and operate at work before meeting Joe. Gaining an understanding of positioning and motivational styles had completely shifted how he perceived others and therefore how he could best work with others. Positioning, Joe had said, is the backdrop to every business interaction, and Don was learning to apply that truth to every business relationship he had. It seemed clear to him that he had been asleep before to the realities of positioning, and as he looked around at others he saw that most were in fact asleep. A few, like Jack, were keenly aware of positioning, and they seemed to be playing an entirely different game from everyone else. In the past, Don would have been tempted to define positioning as "politics," but Joe had helped him realize that positioning is a given drive of human nature, and to ignore it was not noble or high-minded. Rather, choosing to ignore positioning was a common form of ignorance—one that Don had succumbed to.

As a way to gain further insight about competing with Jack, Don asked Joe about the connection between positioning and Power.

"Don't confuse positioning and Power motivation," warned Joe. "Positioning is a constant, like gravity. Positioning happens with all three motivations—Power, Affiliation and Achievement. You could even say that positioning is the screen on which the movie generated by Power, Affiliation and Achievement is played."

Don nodded. He knew that there was a difference, but he also saw that Jack, who was clearly highly motivated by

Power, was very attuned to positioning. He asked for more clarification.

"Think of the differences between Jack and the Boss," suggested Joe. "Both are always positioning for advantage, like all of us. How they do it, and with what intention, however, vary. The Boss sounds like he uses Power for Achievement, while Jack may do the reverse, using his Achievement for Power."

"Yes," Don said. "That makes sense. Jack achieves, and affiliates, in order to satisfy his Power motivation."

"And the Boss uses his Power motivation to achieve," said Joe. "Where positioning comes in is that a good boss positions himself or herself using all three: Power, Affiliation and Achievement."

"Why?"

"Because that is where there is the greatest advantage. Power may be involved in keeping his or her position secure from the constantly circling sharks, Achievement is absolutely vital to keep the money flowing in, and Affiliation keeps people working well together as a team. In fact, where bosses run into problems is when they don't position themselves using all three motivations. Then they typically try to keep things going by rule of law, but people will eventually rebel, reducing production. Or in some cases bosses try laissez-faire strategies that are intended to allow creativity to blossom but end up shielding them so much from the realities of the competitive market that business suffers. Being a good leader means utilizing all three motivations, and delegating well to those who can execute your vision."

Don nodded. He remembered what Joe had said earlier about being a leader, not the lead worker. It was beginning to make more sense. The higher up you go in the organizational hierarchy, the greater need you have for positioning and people management skills. Now that he was seeing the realities of the game more clearly, Don was certain that it was time for him to grow some more, to move into greater challenges and responsibilities.

***

For a summary of this chapter and supplemental material, see page 117.

Chapter 6

BRAND IDENTITY &
THE ANSWER FRAME®

Perhaps he had fallen into the "lead worker" trap that Joe had talked about, when what was really needed was for him to learn how to be a leader. Now it was clear that his new brand purpose had to be for him to become the best leader he could be, which required that he continued learning how to better position himself, how to delegate, and how to really communicate with others to achieve mutual goals.

D on's first order of business after meeting with Joe was to intentionally establish his professional brand identity. He had been to plenty of business seminars and had read countless books on successful management, and so he had naturally heard of branding before, but understanding personal brand identity within the context of positioning made all the difference. As Joe had said, business is all about people because people are the ones making the decisions. Don saw that in one sense he had been trying to take the people out of business, and he thought that this was due to the fact that he had not really understood the game he was actually playing.

To help Don get a quick handle on his personal brand positioning, Joe had given him a worksheet with five headings: Positioning, Purpose, Policy, Product and Procedure. He explained to Don that the "5 Ps" were a forest-to-trees approach, with each level "chunking" down from general to specific. This method, which Joe called The Answer Frame®, guaranteed that there would be complete consistency to the implementation of Don's brand identity. Don sat down and answered the questions at each level.

What is your positioning? Are you one-up, one-down, one-even, or one-apart as it relates to promoting your brand and reputation? What do you have to change to better manage your brand and your customers to gain a better competitive positioning rating in the local wolf pack?

As Don thought about his positioning at BioWidgets, he realized that he had already come quite a distance since he first began working with Joe. He had gone from one-down in regard to his personal brand identity to at least one-even. He credited this to his greater understanding of people's motives, and to his rekindled passion for his work. Indeed Don had come to realize that his former lack of enthusiasm for his job had been in large part a Power and positioning issue. Specifically, he had been over-focused on his own Achievement needs and somewhat blind to his need to position himself as a leader, which included knowing how to communicate better with his reports. He now also saw how his lack of positioning himself had been like handing Jack the promotion without a fight.

As for what he still had to change to gain a better competitive positioning rating, Don thought that he had more to do to be the obvious choice for heading up the new division. Getting the nano-enzyme project back for his team was one goal, and he also thought that he had to press his brand image better to his Boss. The personal branding statement he and Joe had worked out for him was the centerpiece to this effort: A leader and proven research pro who knows the BioWidgets people and culture. That was the brand identity that was going to win him the promotion.

Don read the next set of questions:

> *What is your brand's purpose? To merely "get by"? To be number 1 in your boss's eyes? Or to be a good number 2 in your boss's estimation? To impress the boss and outdo rivals? To be the best _____ (insert appropriate word) who ever worked at Xyz Corporation? To impress a headhunter? To one-up your peers? To impress your family, yourself, or someone else?*

Don thought long and hard about this. His former brand purpose, though he had never thought about it in such terms, was simply to do his job to the best of his ability. While that was something that still appealed to him and his strong Achievement motivation, he realized that it wasn't enough. More accurately, his former definition of his job had been

91

too narrow. Perhaps he had fallen into the "lead worker" trap that Joe had talked about, when what was really needed was for him to learn how to be a leader. Now it was clear that his new brand purpose had to be for him to become the best leader he could be, which required that he continued learning how to better position himself, how to delegate, and how to really communicate with others to achieve mutual goals. Don felt good about all this, even though he knew he was going to need more help to get there.

The next set of questions addressed those communication skills directly:

What is your brand policy about presenting and maintaining your brand image, and how does that affect how you plan your day, your presentations, your projects, your learning curve and your brand promotion strategy?

After Don had thought about this for a few minutes, he realized that his new understanding of his role to his boss was the most significant policy change he had made. Now that he saw his boss as his customer, he was much more proactive in finding out his boss's needs. He was surprised, really, at how easy it had been to transform their relationship: all he did was ask questions. He simply made it a point to ask his boss what he needed, and how he could best help his boss to get things done. Don saw his brand policy, therefore, as asking questions of everyone so that he could implement his brand of being a leader and research pro who understands their corporate culture and the people who make up that culture. As for how that affected his brand promotion strategy, those questions would provide him with the information to create the relationships needed for him to make the winning decisions. As a researcher, he was used to asking questions of the data, and now he would simply extend that approach to more fully include the people he worked with. With his new understandings of motivation, Don now had confidence in his ability to interact and ask questions that would create the rapport he needed to get things done.

He moved on to the next set of questions:

> *What is your primary product or service to your boss? Do you really know what your boss wants and needs from your support efforts – or are you jumping to conclusions without proof? How can you improve that product in terms of your boss, your boss's peers and others? How can you make this brand image better perceived? What don't you know how to do that you need to do to improve your competitive brand?*

Don liked how these personal branding questions led smoothly into each other and forced him to think his work strategies all the way through. For example, this next set of questions made it possible for him to see that his new policy of asking the Boss questions was what had actually made it possible for Don to better understand what his primary service to him was. He used to think that his service to his boss was about coming up with new research ideas and getting projects going to test those ideas. Now he understood that his primary service to his boss had grown into something much more comprehensive than that. It had become clear that what his boss needed from him was for him to take a much more global view and apply his experience and market sense to the upcoming merger. In his review of XYZygote's people, for instance, Don had found that he had a talent for knowing how to put the people jigsaw puzzle together. His boss had been thrilled at Don's first suggestions for how to use their existing teams and integrate them with BioWidgets so that new research could be done that would extend BW's current market reach. In short, Don found that his primary service to the Boss these days was to share his ideas and insights for how to move the merged BW forward into new areas without compromising what they were already doing.

The last set of questions made Don take a careful inventory of how he used his time:

> *What is your day-to-day use of time to promote your brand strategy to the top of the chart? Time is one currency you can't get back. How do you reinforce your brand image with your polished use of telephones, emails, meetings and presentations?*

For a long time it had been no secret to Don that he was not always very good about following up on and responding to email and voice mail messages. Now that he was having more contact with others outside his group, he was beginning to feel overwhelmed. This set of questions, in fact, could not have been timelier. Already he had begun using their group admin more than ever for setting up meetings and making email confirmations, and as helpful as this had been, it was not enough.

Don sat back in his chair and considered all of this in the larger "forest" context of his personal brand. He was branding himself as someone who really knew the BW people and culture, yet here was an essential area of their communication that he clearly had not mastered. His attitude about email and voicemail over the years had been a mixture of passive resistance and relief. The resistance came from all the time he thought that it took up, and the relief was what he often felt when he got someone's voice mail or when he realized that he could simply dash off an email from his phone.

As he considered all of this, Don had to face the fact that his email and voice mail communications were far from the excellence he was working toward in his job. Something had to be done. At this point in the game he couldn't afford to leave any weakness unattended to. He had lost too much time already to Jack. And at the level of Procedure, the branch or twig level of the "forest," he was not in alignment with his personal branding. That, he realized, would have consequences all the way up to Positioning.

Rather than make promises to himself that he might not be able to keep, Don decided to first of all gather some data. He would make a log of emails and voice mails sent and received, and determine just how accurate his sense of the situation matched the reality. From there he would be able to implement the procedures that would have the greatest effect.

For some reason, the decision that Don made to start collecting data on his message communications got him excited. As a researcher and scientist he was a great friend and fan of data, but he had never before considered making himself and his performance a subject for investigation. Each morning he started a new log entry that included the number of emails received overnight, and then he started on his voicemail. What he discovered surprised him, and it gave him some ideas about what to do about managing his message communications. Within a week he thought that he had enough data to start making some efficiency changes, and he started implementing his new procedures with the following email sent to his group:

Subject: New Email Policies

Hello Everyone,

In the interest of better and more efficient message communications in our group, I am requesting that we standardize how and under what circumstances we email each other. First of all, let us agree to make email communication secondary to phone communication. Please reserve email for short, factual exchanges, such as meeting confirmations and information-rich follow-ups to actual phone conversations or face-to-face communication. Email is also appropriate for document forwarding, such as lab reports and technical articles. Also, please use current and specific subject headings.

Regarding voicemail, please take the time to discern whether your communication is more appropriate for email, and also consider whether a lengthy voicemail can actually substitute for a real-time conversation.

Taking a few moments to consider the appropriate form and content of your message will help all of us better manage our message communications.

Let me know if you have any questions about this.

Don E.

What Don had found from his data collection was that somewhere from one-third to one-half of all email he received appeared to be the sender's attempt to avoid personal, real-time communication. This often resulted in multiple emails that stretched over several days, thereby slowing down progress on the matter at hand. Many voicemail messages, as well, appeared to be contact-avoidance voicemail. He caught himself at this several times during the course of his data gathering, and forced himself to avoid leaving long, explanatory messages in favor of a short request that his call be returned as soon as possible.

The result was not only increased productivity, but also a greater sense of connection with his colleagues and co-workers. There also was increased traffic to his office for a short chat about something once he began having more real-time connection with folks, and this led more than once to connections and progress being made that otherwise would have been missed or delayed. All in all, Don had to conclude that the message communications guidelines were leading to a reduction in email and voicemail, which resulted in more face time with others, increased productivity, and a greater sense of personal connection with his team.

***

For a "5 Ps" chart and this chapter's conceptual summary, see page 119.

Chapter 7

BACK IN THE GAME

"And so what has changed? What are you doing differently?"
Joe asked.

As it turned out, somehow the Boss was also alerted to Don's message communications policy, and he brought it up at the next group leaders' meeting. Don was asked to elaborate on the policy and its effectiveness, and the Boss ended up making the policy effective for the entire division. At the meeting's close, Don had the clear sense that the tide had shifted, and that he was back on track for heading up the new research division being formed for post-merger BW. He immediately scheduled a progress report meeting with Casey, and then he called Joe to set up another strategy consultation. Don knew that BioWidgets was going to need that new division to be operational to assist in the merger process, and he wanted to play his best cards over the next weeks so that he could maintain his momentum.

Don was fortunate to schedule a 30-minute phone session with Joe that very evening.

"So," asked Joe, "how are things shaping up?"

Don quickly gave Joe a summary of the day's meeting and said that he felt that he was definitely back in the driver's seat of his career, and that getting the new position seemed more possible than ever.

"Sounds like a good time for us to do a quick review. What has changed for you since we first started talking together?"

"The most important thing," Don replied, "is that I have definitely become a player again."

"What do you mean by being a player?"

"What I mean is that I am definitely back in the game—my team is responding to my directions, my ideas are being implemented division-wide, and I am a strong contender for the leadership position opening up."

"And so what has changed? What are you doing different-ly?" Joe asked.

Don was quiet for a moment. He suddenly remembered the dream that he'd had soon after meeting Joe, the dream about being stuck in the dugout and leaving a huge gap at third base. According to Joe, Don had benched himself, and Joe had been right.

"What has really changed," said Don, "is how I think about my job, and that has changed everything that I do. It's hard to imagine now, but I was really stuck. Because I didn't understand positioning, I had positioned myself into a corner—and I really didn't even know it."

"And now?" Joe prompted.

"Now...," said Don, "now I understand more about why people do what they do, based on their motivations, and this helps me find ways of working together for compatible goals. The short version of it all is that I now know the game I'm in—coopetition—as you call it, and I like it. I like knowing what my goals are, and then figuring out how to get others to help me achieve them in a way that helps them, too. Actually, it's sort of an engineering problem, and now that I know some of the basic principles, I enjoy putting things all together.

"What about Jack?" Joe asked.

"Jack doesn't really matter," said Don. "I'm focused now on being a leader and what leadership is all about, not on Jack.

What I've learned from Jack is that it's okay to try and get ahead. He's been better at it than I've been, but I'm getting the swing of it."

"Sounds to me like you've come a long way," said Joe. "What's next?"

Don paused. He was really so grateful for Joe's guidance over these past months, and he knew that he still had much more to learn from him.

"What's next is that I want to continue positioning myself as strongly as possible for the division leader job."

"Okay," Joe said. "Let's do that."

Timing is everything. The very next morning Don was called in first-thing to the Boss's office, and he was focused and ready. When Don arrived, the Boss extended his hand, and then closed the door behind them. He got right to the point.

"You are on the short list for the division head position. Are you interested?"

***

For supplemental material and this chapter's conceptual summary, see page 122.

Thank you so much for reading *Beyond Office Politics*. As a special offer for our readers, we have arranged for you to get a complimentary Power, Affiliation & Achievement profile.

To participate, go to:
http://www.beyondofficepolitics.com/PAAprofile

COACH'S NOTES

1. Hierarchy & Positioning

There are three types of mammals on the planet:

Solo animals like bears and tigers, which live alone except at mating time.

Herd animals like gazelles, cattle, and sheep that have no social structure.

Hierarchical animals like chimps, apes and humans.

Hierarchical animals, including humans, have an instinct to position themselves as highly in the social system as they can. Much of our stress and conflict is about how we continuously reposition ourselves. Some people don't like to do positioning, some want a better position than they can achieve, some don't want to acknowledge positioning as a fact of life, and some take to positioning like a duck to water.

- Business executives and other professionals are always positioning and repositioning themselves to raise their relative rank.

2. *Power, Affiliation & Achievement*

Power (the need to be in charge and exert influence)
Affiliation (the need to be friendly and cooperative)
Achievement (the need to get things done)

- These motives also define *how* you will play your role in any given context. Conflict often arises from this invisible source when interacting individuals are driven by different kinds of motives.
- Most people have a strong preference for one or two of these motives. Few balance out evenly among the three.
- Differences in motivational emphasis among individuals better explain that the difficulties they have are not of technical substance but of motivational style. Two parties often see reality through different lenses so that the same objective situation looks subjectively different to each of them. Knowing the difference allows one to adjust the way of persuading them.

Power, Affiliation & Achievement Examples

	Star Trek	American Idol
Power:	Kirk	Simon
Affiliation:	Bones	Paula
Achievement:	Spock	Randy

(These are names from the original shows.)

Power, Affiliation & Achievement Exercise

Take 100 points and spread the points around to show how you usually approach most situations:

	You:	Your Boss:
Power	10	70
Affiliation	10	10
Achievement:	80	20
Total (100 points)	100	100

In this exercise example, "you" are low in Power motives and high in Achievement. Your boss is the virtual opposite. This difference in style is a recipe for conflict. If you are mostly Affiliation oriented, you will clash with someone who is mostly Power or Achievement focused. It is in the nature of things. With this insight into the issue of differences, you can apply a little diplomacy and manage the situation effectively.

3. Coopetition® & King Arthur

There is only one of four possible positions that anyone can occupy in any given situation, as demonstrated by *King Arthur's court:*

- One-up: King Arthur is one-up on everyone in the kingdom
- One-down: The knights are one-down to the king.
- One-even: The knights are one-even to each other (they all have the same rank)
- One-apart: Merlin the Magician is one-apart, off to the side, though indirectly part of the system.

The way executives persuasively approach people is very much a matter of how they play the positioning game.

- Depending on whether they are one-down, one-up, one-even or one-apart, calls for adjusting their persuasive techniques.
- Some very effective people are careful to make sure they always appear at least one-even and hopefully one-up on whomever they are trying to persuade.
- By using effective persuasive techniques, one can effectively gain higher perceived rank among others.
- It is a matter of perception: equals tend to treat each other better and assign more credibility to peers than juniors.

- Consultants are often outsiders – one-apart, by definition. Yet consultants are often received as equals or superiors because of their persuasive positioning and persuasive techniques.
- Positioning yourself with persuasive techniques is a big step toward gaining the influence you want.
- As noted before, there are three ways that mammals behave relative to one another: as loners, as part of an amorphous collection with no structure, or as part of a hierarchy. For good reasons, people variously select one of these frameworks as their implicit belief about how they position themselves in relationship to others. Usually, the beliefs they have about this issue are not explicitly conscious.

Power Motivations:

- Good reputation or position
- Status
- Ability to influence others
- Direct, supervise, and control
- Compete against or dominate others

Words and phrases used by people with a high need for Power:

- Control
- Power
- Authority
- Do it my way.

- Now, listen to me.
- I'm the boss.
- It's my decision to make.

Actions to take with Power-motivated people:

- Acknowledge their status, position, or authority.
- Ask for their advice.
- Give them credit for what they do. Acknowledge it.
- Include them in meetings.
- Recognize them publicly.
- Give them authority to act.
- Let them know that they have influenced you.
- Be supportive of their position even when critiquing performance.
- Convince them that doing what you want will get them what they want.
- Keep them up-to-date on all developments.
- Provide symbols of authority.

People with a high need for Affiliation:

- Like to participate as part of a team.
- Need to be liked.
- Need acceptance and positive interpersonal relationships
- Like to work with people.
- Like to minimize conflicts.

Words and phrases used by individuals with a high need for Affiliation:

- Let's get together.
- Team effort / Group effort
- Let's do something for...
- Togetherness
- Help others
- People

Actions to take with people with a high Affiliation need:

- Reward contributions to the group.
- Thank them for helping others get along and work together.
- Demonstrate that you enjoy working with them.
- Recognize the importance of social interactions.
- Smooth over potential conflicts.

People with a high Achievement need:

- Compete against a challenge or standard more than against others
- Set high standards of achievement and/or accomplishment
- Develop new and original ideas and applications
- Set long-range objectives
- Plan for contingencies

Words and phrases used by Achievers:

- Innovative ides
- Eureka, I've got it!
- Let's consider the long term results
- Accuracy
- Planning
- Accomplishment
- Meet plans
- Better than expected

Actions to take with Achievement-motivated People:

- Recognize their achievement through words and/or awards.
- Encourage their initiative and independent thinking.
- Develop job and task structures within which individuals can work toward moderate risk goals.
- Make standards of performance expected by the organization explicit, and provide individuals with concrete feedback relative to their achievement and/or progress in achieving individual and organizational goals.
- Develop an organizational environment in which personal responsibility is encouraged.
- Have them participate in seeking goals and planning target dates.
- Demonstrate appreciation for accuracy and planning.
- Keep projects interesting and challenging.

4. *Your Boss is Your Customer*

Most folks refer to jockeying for the advantages of higher positioning as "politics." But everyone plays politics.

- There are many default versions of politics, such as someone very Achievement oriented getting promoted because of a skill.
- This, the merit theory of upward mobility, leaves all of the control in someone else's hands to decide when the individual has shown merit and when she or he gets to move up.
- Upward mobility is about 80% the results you produce, and 20% self-promotion. If you are not good at managing your brand, your brand being yourself, you can be easily passed over.
- *Opting out of the game of politics is conceding higher positions to those who are willing to play for real.*
- The three spontaneous personality issues that determine how people position themselves are shy, assertive or aggressive. Shy individuals need an indirect approach, assertive types can use an indirect or direct approach as suits them (they are more flexible), while aggressive types tend to prefer a direct approach because it is consistent with their style and Power motives. With the right combination of techniques, however, any one of the three can dominate a situation.

- The indirect approach, skillful questioning, covertly gives you a lot of power because questioning gets the other person talking. That reveals information about how they tick and tells you the scorecard they use to tell they are winning their own version of a WIFM (What's In It For Me). The indirect approach is good for the shy person in particular but also works well for the assertive and aggressive because it is a universally valid approach.

- The indirect approach avoids the bruising aspect of the game by employing *conversational judo* in interpersonal encounters. The cornerstone of this approach is skillful questioning. Because it is less common, few people notice the indirect approach of skillful questioning.

How does the individual avoid disagreement? There are various facets to this answer:

1) Set up your attitude and opening remarks to prevent competitive or argumentative tones and postures i.e., "fighting words" as the pioneers used to call them.

2) Don't inadvertently try to score points at the other person's expense.

3) Try to score for a mutual payoff with the continuous attitude of; "How can I help you?"

5. Business is All About People

Business is often noted for three features: competition, the single-minded pursuit of profit, and sometimes radical, even ruthless, change. These features, however, do not adequately define business. To truly understand the nature of business, we must recognize that **finance**, **technology** and **people** make up the main ingredients of business.

People issues trump finance and technology because people make the decisions for all three. If the situation is good or bad, someone made choices to account for that situation. Business often overrides frames that have to do with cooperation and family values that come at the expense of competition against rivals and profitability. One does cooperate with the home team and compete against the rival team. But often one competes against one's teammates for higher rewards. This conflict among teammates is often a blind spot for those who misconceive colleagues as family members and attempt the ill-conceived "group hug" approach, which always fails except, possibly, in some customer relations.

Religious institutions and Disney films do a great deal to foster an idealized belief in benevolent, often familial relationships of the cooperative sort when, in our culture at least, competition is the dominant form of relationship. So people form beliefs about "how people are supposed to behave," and those beliefs are misplaced in many business contexts with a great deal of debris resulting from the confusion.

Denial of the realities of positioning causes much distress among those who do the denying. Due to the universality of positioning, ***people and rapport skills are fundamental to thriving in business***.

6. Brand Identity & The Answer Frame®

We call the five prevalent framing patterns that one finds commonly in organizations the Answer Frame®. The five patterns are Positioning, Purpose/Motive, Policy, Program/Product (What), and Procedure/Recipe (How).

Positioning: Competitive human situations are always characterized by the instinct of positioning in the local pecking order. We are always in some kind of hierarchical positioning context, even if that context is behind our eyeballs.

What is your positioning? Are you one-up, one-down, one-even, or one-apart as it relates to promoting your brand and reputation? What do you have to change to better manage your brand and your customers to gain a better competitive positioning rating in the local wolf pack?

Purpose/Motive: Within any given context, the individual always has a motive. In the forensic community, wanting (a.k.a. motivation) is central. In other words, if you know what motivates people, you will understand how to influence their behavior in the desired direction. So the question is: "What does the person want within the context of Opportunity and Means?"

What is your brand's purpose? To merely "get by"? To be number 1 in your boss's eyes? Or to be a good number 2 in your boss's estimation? To impress the boss and outdo rivals? To be the best _____ (insert appropriate word) who ever worked at

*Xyz Corporation? To impress a headhunter? To one-up your
peers? To impress your family, yourself, or someone else?*

Policy: (Belief about a class of issues, or a prefabricated
response to a stimulus.) Policy is often the scorecard that one
uses to define the particulars of the motive at hand. Usually
a policy is repetitive in the same way that the production line
of an auto plant repeats its response to getting cars out the
door. If people want to avoid defensiveness, they may have
a policy based upon certain beliefs that they should always
preventatively attack others first. What someone wants has
to be measured or defined as features or benefits if one is to
know that the motive has been achieved. A policy regarding
schoolwork may be that: "It is routine for me to research
my papers more thoroughly than others might so that I will
always produce better term papers than other students in my
graduating class."

*What is your brand policy about presenting and maintaining
your brand image, and how does that affect how you plan your
day, your presentations, your projects, your learning curve and
your brand promotion strategy?*

Program/Product (What): The product or program
may be a series of excellent papers, reports or other products
produced on time and on budget.

*What is your primary product or service to your boss? Do you
really know what your boss wants and needs from your support
efforts – or are you jumping to conclusions without proof? How
can you improve that product in terms of your boss, your boss's*

120

peers and others? How can you make this brand image better perceived? What don't you know how to do that you need to do to improve your competitive brand?

Procedure/Recipe (How): "The way I do research is to run three key words on Google, then take the top three references, then write a paragraph on each, combine the three paragraphs and use that as my project summary. I have other recipes like that one depending on the topic. The content and quality of my writing procedures is top notch. This produces the product/paper that gets me the grades that match my policy that meets my purpose and positions me as top dog."

What is your day-to-day use of time to promote your brand strategy to the top of the chart? Time is one currency you can't get back. How do you reinforce your brand image with your polished use of telephones, emails, meetings and presentations?

7. Back in the Game

Don's success was the consequence of his being able to understand that what was going on in his head did not match the business environment he was in. The value of the right coach or mentor is precisely that—exposing the frame blindness that we all are subject to.

This relates directly to what is called the **Well Formed Outcome**. Whether a thought is well formed or ill formed determines the quality of the decision that follows, as well as its effectiveness. It is often difficult, even impossible, however, for us to gauge the quality of our own thoughts in areas where our beliefs are limiting our ability to make new choices. This is where we need a coach who can elicit the restrictive beliefs and reframe them.

There are four tests that can help you determine whether your goals are real, if you can win with them, and if the results are worth pursuing.

The four tests or conditions of well-formed outcomes (WFO) are:

1) Is the goal stated in the **Positive?** In other words, are you able to state what it is that you want as opposed to what it is you don't want?
2) Is the goal **Ecological?** In other words, are you sure that the goal will not have negative side effects and that it is a win-win goal?

3) Is the goal **Testable**? Can it be tested in material terms? If not, it is a fantasy and not a goal.

4) Is it **Within Your Control**? Taking on a goal you can't call the shots on or pull the strings on will most likely fail.

8. Power, Affiliation & Achievement Profile

Thank you so much for reading *Beyond Office Politics*. As a special offer for our readers, we have arranged for you to get a complimentary Power, Affiliation & Achievement profile.

To participate, go to: www.beyondofficepolitics.com/PAAprofile

Printed in Great Britain
by Amazon